SO MANY
HUMANS,
TOO FEW
RIGHTS

SO MANY HUMANS, TOO FEW RIGHTS

William Manosh

authorHOUSE®

AuthorHouse™
1663 Liberty Drive
Bloomington, IN 47403
www.authorhouse.com
Phone: 1 (800) 839-8640

Published by AuthorHouse 03/26/2018

ISBN: 978-1-5462-3279-7 (sc)

Print information available on the last page.

Contents

Foreword

This book is dedicated to my three awesome children, William II, Jennifer Ashley, and John I Leonard High School Valedictorian princess, Nichole Marie. All of my extra–curricular activities meant my wonderful kids did not have their dads time while he worked tirelessly and attended college.

I also dedicate this book to my lovely wife Cara, and my daughters, Kady and Alexandria for their patience with me these last two years.

List of Tables

I

In-humaneness, Human Rights, and what is Globalization?

Brilliant blocs of international relation organizations, non-governmental organizations (NGOs), and nation- states exist today, and their appreciably pressing missions seem regularly unheard of. They persist consummately, while surrounded by mammoth, opinionated, worldwide, political actors that is to say each other respectively. Currently a complex contemporary western society clashes with eastern ideology vis-à-vis human rights, and how to outline them. The Universal Declaration of Human Rights, proclaimed in 1948 in San Francisco, spearheaded by Eleanor Roosevelt, directed the western version of this remarkable proclamation. Interestingly, and unbeknownst too many, there is also an Islamic version of this same monumental doctrine. That document in no way resembles the western doctrine with the same name. However, a restructured global society should

1

exist by this century, which shows reverence for human rights could be expected, so many of us would think…. right? But, unbelievably, when human rights abuse is considered, we fall way beside the way as a global society. Human rights are not highly respected or upheld anywhere near close to becoming defined as "universal human rights". These human rights have not been protected, or highly developed, and have not been deployed through legal objectives on a global level as evidenced by my research. But, fortunately, they are recognized "universally" by a select few relatively "modern day" NGOs who do say copiously that human rights are to be acknowledged by all nation-states from the eastern to western nations. Their objective is that they should be crystal clarified to every nation state that needs to have them reminded of their seriousness.

These "rights" are astonishing to several bewildered onlookers, but many human rights intellectuals have similar opinions; human rights are not just words written down somewhere in the United Nations Charter, or the Universal Declaration of Human Rights. These profound statements are living in the hearts of the leadership of non-governmental organizations (NGOs). These powerful, privately funded, organizations are willing to go through all necessary means to ensure human rights are realized by people that cannot protect themselves from those who would deny them these rights.

Human rights theory suggests, and it is my politically scientific viewpoint, that these are obligations that nation-states should be required to confer on all of their public figure, without second thought.

The United Nations have supported human rights

enforceability measures from inception, and irradiate accounts of abuses by the authority vested to them under international laws. Regularly, these enforcement measures settle human rights NGO claims of human rights abuse occurrence.

At the end of WWII, the "war to end all wars", the provision to devise and to employ human rights laws, became apparent to scores of alarmed prominent nation-states. The heaving sadistic mayhem, which comprised the well-documented proceedings of the Holocaust, made the situation so profoundly grave, that human rights injustice could not be tolerated bereft of severe repercussions.

United Nations lawmakers, in the course of the credence instituted by the United Nations Charter, developed a modus operandi; this was to thwart and reprimand merciless perpetrators who conducted these outlandish human rights abuses, all the way up to and including genocide.

Human rights abuses are now "illegal acts" under international law, which extends beyond all nation-state boundaries. Nations perpetrating internationally acknowledged human rights abuse with disregard would be held responsible for their bizarre mayhem. Human rights abuses became criminal acts because of this shore up and renewed regard for international law. These new avow would develop into the Rock of Gibraltar for human rights abuse identification. When political scientists begin this discussion regarding universality of human rights, this term globalization will become the topic of discourse. When nation-states, like the United States of America, and supranational organizations, (best exemplified by the United Nations), can benefit human rights the greatest, it's while working amicably with non-governmental organizations. While seeking to execute their job to the fullest, and coexist good-naturedly, their work will always get done in the name of human rights. The underlying reason is not continually evident, and some human rights theorists have been in doubt. However, I feel that it is a simple notion that explains the utmost importance of this association. I suggest it is an all-embracing provision; there is an imperative need to support and expand the development of this relatively new, political scientifically feasible theory, known as globalization. This is the notion that the world is developing a single economy and culture, as a result of improved technology and communications, sparked by the influence of very large multinational corporations. This inevitability is fundamentally an outcome, of the distinctiveness of exceptional, large-scale, international nation states, and their political positioning, having been perpetuated through globalization. Another feasible reason is the prominence leading up to the financial sustainability and implications, which have resulted from the commencing of the legacy and conclusion of the cold war. An insightful political scientist of his time, Peter Van Tuijl argued in one of his more intuitive thesis; "globalization's collision is irregular, and needs to be fit in unity with precise conditions, such as the alleged attrition of the supremacy of nation-states."(Van Tuijl 1999, 2) Where I believe he is going, and I am most agreeable is that there is a wearing away of the complete supremacy, and utter total sustainability, of a nation-state from a globalized perspective. This has obvious implications for human rights. Firstly, progressive global positioning of a nation state economically has without permission or request, made nation states reliant upon others for their existence. Thus this is catapulting them into the worldwide arena of human rights... should I say "like it or not"? The painstaking inquiry into globalization theory simply means that nation states communications on nearly every level have collided with the influence of multinational corporations, and nation states political influences. In turn, there really is no escape from the radar of human rights theory of any particular nation under the umbrella of that nation states international relations theory, for any nation....they cannot escape this periphery. Therefore, negotiations of terms of agreement upon what are acceptable terms of human rights abuses categories, within a nation not only from the nation that are doing "business" will become important, but the opinions of the rest of the world are also just as significant. If country A for example would like to trade with country B, not only does country B have to be in agreement with country A's human rights record, country B has to know that the rest of the world might consider them to be unethical if they are saying that a particular human rights abuse is being committed in nation-state A, yet nation-state B continues to trade or have "talks" with nation-state B anyway. It is a political strategy employed by many nation-states that are onboard with globalization theory that are proponents of human rights. The counter argument will of course be the notion of cultural relativism which will be discussed later in this book. Nation-states that want to tip-toe around human rights abuse and continue to do business with nation-states with dismal human rights records might cite that a nation-state which has a dismal human rights record and just claim it's a part of their culture to practice blatant crimes against other humans. So, if we need their business, we will continue to conduct operations with that nation-state anyways as a nation-state. It is simple, we must survive and perpetuate our priorities. This globalization is a slippery political slope. Nation-states rely upon security of their people to enhance and perpetuate survival of their sovereignty. Human rights and international relations warrant an explanation for why modern human rights dialogue continues to cut like a sharp sword through deep conversations within so many international relations discussions in the name of human rights. Human rights have become progressively more intricate in terms of clarification of a distinct description. There continues to be many unclear human rights abuse descriptive arguments. This book will debate, and continue to outline, an innovative political science approach, to study human rights theory. Hopefully, clarification will come, or at least new questions will form, as we seek to further our quest for answers to this ongoing debate. Political scientists have worn out library book shelves with endless commentary regarding the theory of international relations and human rights.

I needed to calculate the sphere of influence among intercontinental interactions between nation states. While I explored human rights theory further, it was necessary first to identify basic international relations theory's, and discover a consensus as to what human rights theory in fact states that it is. This was difficult because I really could find no concrete or operational/functional definition other than that definition found in the Encarta dictionary: 1. Of people, relating to, involving, or characteristic of human beings, human nature, human frailty, 2. Made up of people, composed of people, the human race, a human chain, 3. Compassionately kind, showing kindness, compassion, approachability, 4. Imperfect, having the imperfections and weaknesses of a human being.

Given this to work with, I knew I was treading new ground with this work. The study of political science and international relations frequently will lead you to believe that the progress or representation of a preliminary position which would help explain a "simple" human rights theory is not available across cultures.

Conversely, it is straight away unmistakable, that human rights theory does not develop or match up precisely with the two prevailing westernized international relations theories such as the realist and idealist international relations theories. To help solve these perplexities, the light at the end of the tunnel, and the real purpose of this book was to scrutinize intensely, utilizing political science research methods, the intricate nature of international NGO activism campaigns. Typically, I discovered that the countries cited for various human rights violations were, and some still are, going through various states of economic and political stabilization, post de-colonization. However, this is not true for every nation. Those still with the most citations are those particular nations more often than not, who receive the most observation and endure the most scrutiny and criticism. In turn this appears to result mainly from the inability to balance new regime stabilization and human rights simultaneously.

However, there are likely many more variables to be tested to prove this to be entirely true. Further investigation did reveal that this is not always the case. NGOs are well organized, but many would consider them to be a maze of policy networks, with their unique goals in mind; which are to further the mission of their individual organizations, as well as pursue their main priority; to quickly eradicate human rights atrocities.

The primary difficulty for human rights scholars, political scientists, and so many uninformed nation state citizens, is that public opinion does not often have an influential role within this particular dissertation. So the communications being guided by the NGOs are not always received by those intended regarding human rights abuse.

Human rights abuses are frequently perceived as a case of relativity to a nation states own political, social, cultural, economic, and civil rights perspectives. I call this notion "relativity of rights." This is also frequently referred to as cultural relativism. This notion proves to be troublesome for a universal definition of human rights theory as well as a definition of a universal theory of international relations from a western standpoint. Simplified further, western governments may have to treat other nation states differently based upon their cultures, as human cultures are variable and are dealt with on a case by case basis. Exceptions have been allowed based upon cultural relativism between nation states regarding human rights abuses. International relations experts argue as well as NGOs and political scientists about these theories. If this is the way to handle international relations with non-compliant nation-states, it does appear to be inconsistent with morality and ethics which should be universal. However, nation states must pursue relations regardless oftentimes. Many of these reasons are likely kept confidential from the public figure. How are human rights, NGO's and international relations inter-connected? In this book I chose to analyze the human rights missions of three powerhouse human rights NGOs. Through an up-to-the-minute political science research method called "content analysis", I deployed my reading of United States Congress resolutions that mentioned specifically in the resolution the terminology for "human rights." These were outlined specifically in the language contained in many of the resolutions presented in the US Congress from the 101st Congressional session through the 108th session. This period covers the post-cold-war era period between 1989 through 2004. I characterized this part of the research as a longitudinal study. This fifteen year period, had several reoccurring human rights abuses related to congressional resolutions introduced in the United States Congress. There was a tremendous amount of activity not really much to my surprise, but unusually more than I had anticipated. Naturally, numerous activism campaigns citing the same countries occurred simultaneously by the three NGOs chosen. My research goal, ultimately, in part, was to look for, and give explanation if there was some category of relationship, a nexus, or undeviating correlation, that had been sifted out of the dialogue between the US Congress human rights related resolutions, and the NGO activist campaigns citing human rights abuse during that particular session of Congress. Activist campaign information for all three NGOs chosen for this book, and their campaigns were not completely available for assessment dating back to the 101st Congress. I did not let this be a problem for the study. So, nevertheless I used the information from the NGO activist archives as early as it was available to enhance the comparison. To further enhance my inquiry, a case- study political science approach helped provide a detailed examination of the NGOs perspective of human rights abuse. Operational designation for human rights for the NGOs chosen, were developed through comparison of human rights abuse policies and procedures for each NGO. An assessment of the preparatory tasks that helped form the notion of human rights was crucial for the outcome of this book. I researched the words and substance of the Universal Declaration of Human Rights (UDHR), proclaimed in 1948, in San Francisco to make certain this notion of human rights was distinctive, telling, and as reverent as I had already known it to be. Various covenants and countless agreements sponsored by the United Nations had advanced my "relativity of rights" notion. The much debated notion coined cultural relativism kept sifting its way to the top. The operational definition for human rights is not for infinity, evident crossways between nation states government policy's, lawmaking organizations, or amid NGOs in broad-spectrum. However, when I compared what I felt were attempted scholarly definitions for human rights theory, to prevailing international relations idealist and realist theory, was it imperative to simplify a definition for human rights theory? This helped me to follow a less complex line of investigation for this book. As I researched for all intents and purposes, I made a comparison of time-honored prevailing international relations theories, with liberal based, human rights theory. After this inquiry, it was necessary to compare the results. I concluded that it is apparent there is a need for a more decidedly advanced method to progress the review of human rights, for the reason that this perplexity of a human rights theory definition coincides with the progression of worldwide democratization. This notion, in turn, also advances prevailing western human rights explanation and description. So the next intricacy is how to decide which international relations theory should be applicable, as you decide to launch one in defense of your position of human rights abuse in each particular nation state. Given this, this new information appears to further complicate an easier to understand explanation for what I hoped to begin to further simplify. Do international relations theories apply only from a westernized standpoint? Does the same hold true for human rights theory? This evidence should sift to the top upon further reading. Can globalization indeed tie western and eastern civilizations cultures together? These and so many additional new questions will advance this content from the groundwork that I have put forth in this book. I will hope that the readers take the study seriously and perhaps draw some useful conclusions of their own. What is it exactly that forms the magnet that draws the United States Congress and NGOs together? The NGO subjects of this 15 year longitudinal case study were Amnesty International (AI), Human Rights Watch (HRW), and Human Rights First (HRF), formerly known as Lawyers Committee for Human Rights. While utilizing political science research methods, I gathered evidence by way of the content analysis method, to demonstrate if activism campaigns conducted by each NGO reflect the same distinction of human rights issues, as the human rights issues simultaneously recorded in the respective congressional resolutions while Congress was in session. To reiterate, the primary intention of this book is to discover significant, convincing evidence, whether the United States Congress was solely reliant upon human rights NGOs, or were there perhaps some other sources utilized, when they identified and acknowledged human rights problems? The US Congress then proposed law making decisions known as congressional resolutions related to human rights abuse domestic, and abroad. The period of time looked at thoroughly and analyzed for this study, is the post-cold-war era. It was my hypothesis that the most important issues for these human rights groups, could overlap concurrently with congressional resolutions in the respective congressional sessions. Human rights NGOs expend great time, energy, and resources to identify various human rights abuses that they determine to be of international concern. This diligent effort and dedication to human rights advancement, while closely observing international law, had to have been demanding. Because the US Congress represents the peoples branch of the government, political scientists could also theorize human rights abuses would likely be salient issues to the American people. But has this actually been the case? The political scientists who specialize in the study of Congress, Kenneth B. Mayer and David T. Canon persuade in their book, "that a core of the argument Madison set out in Federalist 10 is that larger constituencies would be more likely to focus on national issues, and smaller constituencies to show undue concern with local interests." (Canon and Mayer 1999, 6) Congress does often take special consideration with matters abroad, even when there are salient matters for their constituents that may often appear to take preference in a collection of voting conditions; such as near an upcoming election. Suitable to America's vast multicultural range, "the melting pot," I expect that the US Congress does distinguish which human rights issues abroad would be critical to public opinion as well as the American people's domestic issues. This was unmistakable, at least in fraction, in the course of the outcome of the content analysis, regarding the diverse human rights abuses, that became the focus of a congressional resolution that were revealed in my research. NGOs have a great deal of crucial effectiveness as human rights concerns stir up dissent in the US Congress. They are opinionated human rights observers, self-governing as intergovernmental organizations, that brandish tremendous supranational persuade. The most salient issues revealed within the frequent reoccurring congressional resolutions, usually elicit instantaneous foreign policy repercussion. Hence, the economic, political, cultural, civil and social rights of potential economic partners and nation-states allies worldwide give rise to inconceivable evidence of the implication of this conclusion.

II

Brief History of
Human Rights

A mountain of research into human rights has been piloted by human rights scholars, political scientists, and international relations lawyers. Human rights are at times, highly debated and often mostly divisive topics. The vast amount of human rights historic and current literature, necessitates a worthy research strategy, from start to finish. In this book, the history of human rights, is every much as important as the present day discourse, while discussing their seriousness.

As early, as 1740 B.C.E. there is evidence to suggest that human people had some "types" of rights. In Babylonia, a rival Mesopotamian kingdom, some laws and codes are located on a clay tablet "to establish justice throughout Mesopotamia". "The code of Hammurabi survives in a stone column discovered in Iran in 1901 and is now located in Paris". (University of Minnesota, Human Rights

Timeline, 6) Many scholars propose this to be one of the world's oldest lawful credentials.

The Treaty of Westphalia, signed in 1648, is also a recognized source of natural rights law. This period of the historic timeline placed the king at the head of the Catholic Church. "The treaty of Westphalia freed states from the jurisdiction of the Catholic Church". (University of Minnesota, Human Rights timeline, 6)

John H. Jackson, a prominent political scientist in his day, considers this lengthy document to be a "Peace Treaty between the Holy Roman Emperor, the King of France, and their respective allies." (Jackson 2003, 786) Over time, the theory of 'Westphalia sovereignty', talked about by Jackson, developed into important notions of the absolute rights of a sovereign nation. The treaty became a momentous foundation of the importance of nation-state sovereignty. All too familiar, but equally as important in human rights history, is the United States Declaration of Independence, proclaimed in 1776. The implications for basic human rights found within this historical masterpiece, would come to influence modern western thought and the formal notion of all human rights, for centuries to come, and to this day. "Thomas Jefferson theorized much to the same ideology as "natural rights" theories first introduced by Locke and Montesquieu". "This monumental constitutional declaration accused King George of tyranny, announced the colonies separation from Great Britain, and proclaimed the creation of the United States". (University of Minnesota, Human Rights Timeline, 6)

To account for far-eastern human rights contemplation, it is equally important to recognize an important human rights philosopher named Confucius. Confucius lived in a politically and socially unstable period in the Far East from 551- c. to 479 B.C.E. His philosophy was concerned with social and government reforms. The idea of "jen" educated a theory of benevolence expressed in terms of "do not do to others what you would not like yourself". "Do unto others what you wish to do unto yourself". These incredible revelations are closely associated with individual rights and responsibilities. His teaching also became a code of conduct for Chinese citizens and a basis for a way of life. "Government, in Confucius view, should practice "jen" rather than use force." (University of Minnesota, Human Rights Timeline, 6) Political scientists and scholars of history have also found text relating directly to human rights; in the Old Testament of the Holy Bible dating 1200- 300 B.C.E. Another often overlooked source document for the notion of human rights is the New Testament of the Christian Holy Bible. However, it is not often cited in terms of human rights historical documents. The period c. 40- 100 C. E. reveals the life of the prophet Jesus. To best illustrate this example you must analyze the content of his interesting and benevolent doctrine. The New Testament says that Jesus taught that "rights come together with responsibilities". (University of Minnesota, Human Rights Timeline, 6) Jesus Christ teachings espouse the rights of humans as rights and as responsibilities. Is it important to recognize human rights historical and religious implications found in these teachings as part of the culmination of present human rights doctrine? Christians would argue yes it is. Fast forwarding to the 20th century, the prominent political scientist Horst Dippel's analysis suggests that the French Declarations of

1789, 1793, and 1795 embody a close up affiliation, which exists between individual rights and the general interest of society. According to some French political science opinion, individual rights and interests are legitimate only as long as they do not contradict public rights and interests. "Individuals enjoy their human rights not by natural world but as part of the society as a whole". (Dippel 1996, 32) Dippel's argument is that in the French understanding, society assumed practically the role of an intermediate power between government and the individual.

The obvious conclusions drawn from Dippel's analysis of the French Declarations are that rights are not in alienable, but individuals do have rights as a collective nature within the umbrella of a society. This collective nature of rights places emphasis on the nation state or on society in general. However, the real emphasis is still that individuals do have rights. As significant as this interpretation is, even more significant is the fact that these are references to the concept of human rights. The French Declaration is noteworthy to understanding the French historical implications of human rights. Many other significant quotes which contain connotations of early human rights theory are also paramount to understanding where we stand today in Europe and the rest of the world. Modern human rights dialogue can be attributed to theories and quotes made by our famous leaders Abraham Lincoln, and Theodore Roosevelt. In addition, the notion of idealism which is often closely associated with human rights discourse, can be attributed to the likes of President Woodrow Wilson and columnist Sidney Hudson Harrison. Basler quotes President Lincoln in a speech at Chicago, Illinois in the summer of 1858, "I believe that each individual is naturally entitled to do as he pleases with himself and the fruit of his labor, so far as it no wise interferes with any other man's rights that each community, as a state, has a right to do exactly as it pleases with all the concerns within that state that interfere with the right of another state, and that the general government, upon principle, has no right to interfere with anything other than that general class of things that does concern the whole." (Basler 1953, 493) President Lincoln is long winded with this quote but you can see where he is going. Human rights are important as ever to this historic figure. Former president Theodore Roosevelt spoke eloquently with a hint of favorability of human rights in Paris, France in the spring of 1910, "My position as regards the monies interests can be put in a few words. "In every civilized society, property rights must be carefully safeguarded ordinarily and in the great majority of cases, human rights and property rights are fundamentally and in the long run identical; but when it clearly appears that there is a real conflict between them, human rights must have the upper hand, for property belongs to man and not man to property." (The work of Theodore Roosevelt 1926, 515-516) It is clear where President Roosevelt stood regarding human rights from this quotation.

Shaw quotes President Woodrow Wilson who takes an idealist tone in a speech to support the League of Nations in the fall of 1919. "America is the only idealistic nation in the world." (Shaw 1924, 822) President Wilson was also a political scientist and our most highly educated president. He was responsible for the formation of the League of Nations as well.

Landers quotes Sidney Harrison in the Chicago Sun

Times in his column entitled Thought at Large, "An idealist believes the short run doesn't count. A cynic believes the long run doesn't matter. A realist believes that what is done or left undone in the short run determines the long run." (Landers1979, B7) These famous quotations further emphasize how history has shaped modern human rights discourse and policies. These brilliant people spoke eloquently regarding the importance of human rights and idealist ideology. These points are extremely relevant to research involving human rights theory as it relates to dominant international relations theories. My hypothesis is that these two types of theories are interrelated and thus inseparable. When a political scientist must mention a particular international relations theory, as well as human rights theory, the human rights theory will frequently contain many differences in identification and ideology when compared to internationally excepted international relations theories. This fact in my strong opinion is due to cultural relativism. Therefore, it can be assumed that no single human rights theory can exist separate from any given international relations theory. This can only spell out difficulties for international relations; NGOs work in general, and the theory of globalization. My research for this book has enhanced this notion further as you will see when you read on.

III

The United Nations Charter and The Universal Declaration Of Human Rights

If their is one thing political scientists share and agree upon it is the inherent strengths and weaknesses of the wording found within the United Nations preamble. However, let this not be a stumbling block as this is a monumental historic document. "We the peoples of the United Nations determined to reaffirm faith in fundamental human rights, in the dignity and worth of human beings, in the equal rights of men and women and of nations large and small." (United Nations Human Rights Website, 1) The preamble language affirms that the government's delegates had agreed to the wording of the United Nations Charter on that infamous day in the city of San Francisco, California. This was one of the most significant acts of world unification and diplomacy to be orchestrated that century. For the sake of understanding what this establishment really means to the notion of human rights, it is important to comprehend fully the exact wording in the preamble related to human rights as they later come to be legally and morally defined by various NGOs and the United Nations. My research convincingly confirms the notion that there really is no definition of human rights found within the preamble of the United Nations Charter and for good reason. It is difficult to imagine which countries could have agreed upon a definition for human rights abuses at that time? Furthermore, if a country was not willing to ratify this treaty, they could miss the opportunity to become a member of the United Nations. Arguably, this was the biggest integration of friendship among nations to become available to weaker countries as well as the most powerful countries in the world. The first opportunity was of course membership in the United Nations. The political, economic, social, cultural, and civil implications of such an elite fraternal membership of countries presented new opportunities for many countries that would preserve power for those elite countries and give power to those without inherent power.

The United Nations Charter entered into force in January 1942. Twenty-six countries proclaimed their belief that victory in World War II was essential to preserve human rights and justice in their own lands as well as in other lands. A prominent political scientist Paul Gordon Lauren discusses in his essay that almost exactly one-year earlier President Roosevelt in a speech to the US Congress had said emphatically "Freedom means the supremacy of human rights everywhere." (Lauren 1983, 4) This particular human rights discourse stemmed arguably at that time from the mayhem of conflict. Genocide because of ethnic intolerance was one of the most blatant human rights abuses to have occurred in modern time. These human rights issues were so relevant that scholars like Woodrow Wilson, who had previously introduced the League of Nations, and presidential heroes like Roosevelt would pave the way towards a boulevard of harmony. This was in direct opposition to taking a path of national isolation which the United States has also considered. Both leaders recognized that political alliances and coalitions with these historic organizations, that transcend national sovereignty and could strengthen and maintain power for the United States and improve diplomatic relations with her allies abroad. The political scientist Clark Eichelberger published a relevant viewpoint in a scholarly journal that discusses extensively with reference to the early successes and alliances formed by the United Nations just shortly after becoming an organization. He goes on to say "talking about the Russians in 1947", "they wanted a United Nations that would really be a Security Council presided over by four or five great powers, with adequate military forces behind it to restrain regression." (Eichelberger 1947, 98) I believe that he is partially correct in this statement and it is important to realize his analysis is during the decade that these events take place. The United Nations had extended an invitation to the Soviet Union even though they had opposed the allies concerning what to do with Germany at the end of that horrendous war. Ideologically, the western powers and allies were not in agreement with Marxist philosophy. However, the severity of the atrocities, and the immediate need to unite against human rights abusers, would unite countries that could have otherwise presented more tribulations for the allies in the diminutive period. This could very well have been the Soviet Union. Taking into consideration the tension and scars left after the wars end, the United Nations became an international representation of collaboration and agreement. Insofar as the UN Charter is concerned with human rights and fundamental freedoms, (Articles 1, 3; 55, C; 62, 3; 76, C), as well as the preamble, there is recognition of an individual's place in the international order as well.

Carl J. Friedrich, a well-respected political scientist of that era proposed his argument in defense of the UN Charter, "Conquest and imperialism are incompatible with a world order" (Friedrich 1947, 28). Friedrich's analysis is in line with what the world had seen left by conquest, and is quick to point out that the United Nations Charter is a long way from achieving peace, but is a step into the right a direction.

The outspoken political scientist Eichelberger reflected on the "present machinery" and indicated that he has hope with some reasonable expectations for the United Nations. He goes on to quote Senator Austin the American delegate on the Security Council who is speaking to a conference of state governments, "the resources of the United Nations Charter and the capacity for growth of the United Nations are limited only by our ability to use them."(Eichelberger 1947, 98) His investigation is important to this book because it represents the early scholarly thought regarding human rights discourse and the formation of the United Nations. The most salient issues at that time were money, airplanes, food, health, and trade. There was an International Court of

Justice established as well which would become paramount to things to come in the 21st century. Unfortunately, the vagueness of the United Nations charters descriptive language, would propel renewed attempts to define human rights further as well as the ensuing discourse shortly after Eichelberger's publication. Eichelberger has reservations obviously, but I feel it is important to see his analysis clearly for this book as his publication is very nearly written close to the time period after the United Nations was formed. Moreover, supplementary to the historical importance of his publication I suggest that without delay, even as an outsider, he had recognized what many others had realized was crucial. There were numerous valid implications by scholarly fellowship, that more specific terms would have to take the place of morally weighty terminology so vaguely identified as human rights in the United Nations charter. My exploration for purposes of this argument is to advocate that this is a perfect example and an explanation for the requirement of a liberal understanding of human rights. This imperative response so gladly looked forward too, would be on the way soon. This became the newest and one of the most renowned human rights citations to have ever been proclaimed.

Fortunately, to supplement the vagueness and non-descriptive mentions of human rights in the UN Charter, a preamble was drafted known as the Universal Declaration of Human Right (UDHR). Proclaimed on December 10, 1948 by the General Assembly of the United Nations, it is an outline of articles which represent a thorough, but unfortunately, not universally accepted definition of human rights. This is manifested by some Middle Eastern nation states that have drafted their own Universal Declaration of Human Rights. Although it is not a binding treaty, it represents a definition, a starting point, a reference and a symbol of what human rights ought to be with great influence by the chair of the drafting committee, Mrs. Eleanor Roosevelt. These were painstaking human rights, clearly outlined, inherent to all human beings inalienable and without exception by virtue of being born. The UDHR is also often scrutinized to be a mirror image of romanticism and the normative theory of how nation-states should treat their people. The preamble of the UDHR mentions fundamental human rights and a reaffirmation by the United Nations to recognize them. Equally as important is the fact that the preamble wishes to promote universal respect for and observance of human rights and fundamental freedoms. (The Universal Declaration of Human Rights, 1) "The preamble expressly mentions this declaration as a common standard of achievement for all peoples and all nations, to the end that every individual and every organ of society, keeping this declaration constantly in mind, shall strive by teaching and education to promote respect for these rights and freedoms and by progressive measures, national and international, to secure their universal and effective recognition and observance, both among the peoples of member states themselves, and among the peoples of territories under their jurisdiction." (Universal Declaration of Human Rights, 1) This colossal doctrine has of course some flaws to consider. It does significantly contradict itself by indicating in the first sentence to be a common standard for all people and all nations. However, it concludes with a contradiction that the document includes peoples of member states and territories under their jurisdiction. From a legal point of view under international laws perhaps, this notion invites disagreement. If a person has their human rights violated and their nation-state is not a member or a signatory of the UDHR, they are not protected under the UDHR? This seems troublesome to me. The UDHR preamble does not legally bind member states and non-member states under international law or the doctrine of tradition or custom under international law rules. However, the UDHR has been cited to be a custom because several nation-states recognize and adhere to its doctrine. This is extremely significant because the International Bill of Human Rights and almost all other formal human rights related treaties have recognized the Articles within the UDHR with the precise human rights language it contains. With this being the case, it would suggest that any person who had their human rights violated would indeed be covered under the provisions of the UDHR. This indeed is the good news!

Reoccurring themes and special significance given to particular nation-states human rights violations, have varied and for understandable reasons. The UDHR proclamation was drafted during a particularly troublesome political and social turbulence occurring all over the world. However, this would not be the only western tie to the defining articles found within the UDHR. The human rights discourse contained within the articles can effortlessly be debatably a mirror of the times, and a genuine idealistic depiction of privileges that every man woman and child would expect to have the benefit of while existing on this earth. It is easier to explain the meaning of the articles if they are divided categorically. Five categories of rights comprise the UDHR.

They are civil, political, economic, social, and cultural rights. The first two articles describe the entitlement to all of the rights by virtue of being born free. The second article discusses the fact that there can be no discrimination against anyone for any reasons. Articles 3-18 are the civil group of rights, these articles are defined as personal freedoms of a member of a society. The political rights are located within articles 19-21. The economic, social and cultural rights are covered within articles 22-27. Articles 28-30 contain language relating to the right to self-determination of peoples, the requirement and limitations of human rights for an individual in a community. A strict prohibition of human rights culminated with Article 30. (Abbreviated Version of the UDHR, 1) When compared with excepted international relations theories, once again this theory of human rights contains traces of global international relations and shows traces of the realist theory of international relations. Together the articles in this proclamation have strengthened already sturdy cultures; and in theory, could also have preserved indigenous, deprived cultures. The UDHR has led to numerous enforced covenants among nations, and has improved politically perceived weakness and breakdown in human rights behavior since its inception. It has been a model, a reference, and a starting point for humanity to consider as being imperative to consider as they reach out to struggling nation states personage.

IV

Scholars Speak Up the Topic: United Nations

The Commission on Human Rights convened near the beginning of 1946. According to the International Bill of Human Rights: the International Covenant on Economic, Social, and Cultural Rights and the International Covenant on Civil and Political Rights were adopted by the General assembly by its resolution 2200A (XXII) of 16 December, 1966.

The first optional protocol to the International Covenant on Civil and Political Rights, adopted by the same resolution, provided international machinery for dealing with interactions from individuals claiming to be victims of violations of any of the rights set forth in the covenant. (United Nations Fact Sheet No. 2 Rev 1 1996, 4) What does this mean in terms of the United Nations contributions to human rights? A considerable amount of effort has helped achieve a pinnacle of human rights legislation through the efforts of the United Nations. This effort has culminated with the establishment of the International Bill of Human

Rights (United Nations Fact Sheet No. 2 Rev 1 1996, 4). The International Bill of Human rights contains several protocols. These protocols consist of the UDHR, the International Covenant on Economic, Social and Cultural Rights, the International Covenant on Civil and Political Rights, the Optional Protocol to the International Covenant on Civil and Political Rights and the Second Optional Protocol to the International Covenant on Civil and Political Rights aiming at the abolition of the death penalty. (UN Fact Sheet No. 2 rev1 1996, 4)

The 1966 covenants had provided two types of human rights protection. Civil and political rights were the emphasis in the first protocol. Political, economic, and cultural human rights are emphasized in the second protocol. What these covenants did accomplish importantly enough, was a provision for legal machinery to deal with international claims of victims of any human rights abuses that had been set forth within these particular covenants. (United Nations Fact Sheet No. 2 1996, 4)

Both covenants entered into force in the spring of 1976. As of 1995, each covenant contained 132 countries. (United Nations Fact Sheet No. 2 1996, 13) The United States did ratify both covenants. However, interestingly enough, as of 2004 the US had not ratified either optional protocol one or two. Optional protocol one contained provisions that the United Nations Human Rights Committee could receive claims made by one states victim against another and act competently. Eighty-five states did agree to have these claims heard by the committee for human rights at the United Nations. The International Covenant on Civil and Political Rights also contains optional protocol number two.

The second protocol is related to provisions to abolish the death penalty. Twenty-eight states did ratify that optional protocol. (United Nations Fact Sheet No.2 Rev 1 1996, 15) As most of my readers know the United States is still one of the proud nation states that bolster capital punishment.

Many scholars agree that the International Bill of Human Rights represents one of humankind's greater achievements. It is not a failure to stop atrocities to humanity before they occur. However, unfortunately, not everyone is pleased with the implications of universal human rights because some nation-states view human rights as an obstacle to the principles of nation - state sovereignty. This has at times been problematic for powerful countries that do not wish to give up economic, political, social, civil or cultural rights to smaller, some less economically fortunate nation-states.

The role of the United Nations and the United States should be paved clear regarding human rights but these two organizations do not always see the world through the same international relations lenses. Strong evidence for this was discovered through content analysis of numerous US Congressional resolutions where it was discovered that the United States has made mention of withdrawing completely from the United Nations several times since 1989. Some academia's suggest that human rights theory is particularly problematic not only for nation-states but for all those agencies and governments directly affected. The more common theory problems involve the universality of human rights. It is still a strong matter of debate whether human rights can be truly "universal" by definition. Cultural relativism, international relations, and international law, often propose conflicting views with human rights theory at various levels of analysis. For example, countries that are still de-colonizing this century are particularly vulnerable to civil, political, economic, social, and cultural notions of human rights within their territories. The five main human rights categories have not come to fruition in a number of third world countries. This fact is arguably largely due in great part to those countries recent evolution as sovereign territories. The arguments and disagreement with universal human rights is usually the same, state governments respond that these rights do not apply to them because we do not recognize them to be important to the sovereignty of our state. This has been particularly problematic.

Furthermore they have argued that why should they have to recognize human rights if they have never recognized them as a part of their culture? The implications include recognizing that western ideological human rights do not mirror the same political, cultural, social, economic, and civil rights as eastern ideological human rights. Additionally many middle eastern civilizations, as well as many African colonies the have recently formed statehood do not mirror western ideologies. Some of these cultures out date some western civilizations literally by centuries.

Scholars, nation- state leaders, and less civilized militias have opposing views regarding human rights, so it is difficult to get a consensus related to cultural relativism and universality of rights. The opposing themes reoccur and are always related to the universality of human rights, the enforcement mechanisms to punish violators, international laws, and to the leaders of those governments and their states sovereignty. Meantime the economic and political implications for the US are frequently unbalanced by and challenged in the name of the perpetual human rights machinery. The US has to make preparations for its own economic future while deciding how to interact with countries that do not respect, and literally disregard, basic human rights doctrine contained in human rights treaties as well as the UDHR. These complicated issues can be traced to the articles within the language of the UDHR, which have aided immeasurably to the drafters of the various covenants and now serve as legal agreements between some nations. Unfortunately some other nations remain unbound.

Nation states have had a plentiful amount of work to accomplish when they decide how to implement international human rights policies. Local human rights deficiencies call for reforms that would address the complexity and particularity of each human right.

Cyril Adjei, renowned political scientist in his field suggests that the social constructivist viewpoint suggests that it is both liberal theorists and critical legal scholars that share the statutory protection of human rights. (Adjei 1995, 28) In his perspective, human rights are contingent in the sense that they reflect values that a given community considers to be fundamental. This view partially explains how complex the notion of fundamental human rights really is. The first round debate is that human rights doctrine is often contradicting and especially difficult for legal analysis. Furthermore, human rights doctrine is especially difficult for critical legal analysis largely a result of the vagueness of the relevant statutes, as well as applicability to each nation state. Scholars have had their "hands full" with competing views and must rely heavily upon previous case law and what is the significance of business with that particular nation?

"Community standards" have been frequently applied to US judicial language when interpreting the applicability of various laws at various levels of government. Human rights legal scholars have taken this approach as well, in hopes of determining the best arguments under international law jurisdiction, to defend or prosecute human rights abuses. Often contrasting with those laws are defense mechanisms built in to the UN Charter which are frequently cited in defense of a state's domestic sovereignty.

Famed for his relevant point of view regarding the United Nations, Alexander J. Pollock enlists a theory of conservative jurisprudence in which he "interprets the role of the United Nations in the South West Africa Cases with emphasis on Article 2, section 7 of the United Nations Charter. This Article indicates that "nothing in the present charter shall authorize the United Nations to intervene in matters that are essentially within the domestic jurisdiction of any state or shall require the member to submit such matter for settlement under the present Charter."(Pollock 1969, 770) Pollock contends that under international law, the United Nations is a group of sovereign nations. If these states express their opinion on some matter it tells one nothing but that the majority of nations have that opinion. Therefore, its declarations and resolutions cannot legally bind a sovereign state, and the fact that they express a different moral evaluation of racial discrimination or separate development is without legal importance. (Pollock 1969, 770) It is safe to conclude that Pollock's publication regarding the South West Africa Cases is not in tune with customary international law principles. Why does he take the excessive arrangement in opposition to the United Nations Charter? Pollock is taking the literal critical human rights scholarly approach with an obvious exception to the phrasing of human rights ruling set up within the various doctrines.

His critique also mentions that there is apprehension regarding the United Nations Declaration on the Inadmissibility of Intervention in the Domestic Affairs of States and the Protection of Their Independence and Sovereignty. He argues that in these declarations, it states expressly "every state has an inalienable right to choose its political, economic, social, and cultural systems, without interference in any form by another state." However, it then goes on to say, "all states shall respect the right to self-determination and independence of peoples and nations, to be freely exercised without any foreign pressure and with absolute respect to human rights and fundamental freedoms". (Pollock 1969, 770)

I know it may seem like I am picking on Pollock here but his point of view declares that the United Nations defines a state to be sovereign and then allows interferences with its domestic decisions under certain circumstances. This is an excellent example once again, of analysis that portrays contradictory language in human rights doctrine found within the UN Charter. This will of course have obvious implications for all international human rights actors, national elites, and nation-states.

Within an anonymous publication by E.H.C. obtained from a political science journal they conclude that "the unanimous decision of the California District Court of

Appeals in Fuji v. State has caused wide comment both in the press and in legal periodicals. This court held that the Alien Land Law, which prohibits aliens who are ineligible to become citizens from owning land, to be unenforceable as against the United Nations and the Declaration of Human rights. "This is the first time that a court in the United States has used the Charter of the United Nations and the Declaration of Human Rights to invalidate a state law." (E.H.C. 1950 1059) This article which was taken from the Virginia Law Review outlines the author's disbelief that a supranational charter could change national domestic law. However, in this case it did. In 1950, the UDHR, somehow, had a far reaching hand into domestic land law. Today, it is uncertain that this document still contains this type of domestic jurisdiction. According to Lawrence Finkelstein, known for his UN expertise, "the concept of domestic jurisdiction" embodied in Article 2, paragraph 7 of the UN Charter, has frequently been criticized both on the ground that it is an undesirable limit on United Nations jurisdiction, and on the ground that the language of the Charter did not sufficiently inhibit incursions by United Nations organs, especially the General Assembly, into matters which should remain of purely national concern." (Finklestein) 1955, 222) Peace and security are Finklestein's principal concern. His quarrel proposes that the United Nations is incapable to execute its obligation to the peace in my opinion is unjustified by the language contained in Article 2 paragraph 7 of the UN Charter. The discourse during the continuous evolution and implementation of human rights covenants and treaties has been diverse and regularly unhinged.

The finest analysis procedure for scholars to take is to determine the facts on a case-by-case basis, and then formulate decisions given all applicable information. These scholarly questions represent the resulting growing pains that scholars, nation-states, and the United Nations have had to identify, work through, and interpret during relentless human rights dissertation involving states sovereignty and universal human rights interpretations as well as there implementation.

V

Amnesty International, Activism, and getting it done!

Amnesty International (AI) defines itself as a worldwide movement of people who campaign for internationally recognized human rights. (About Amnesty International 2004, 9) Wherever your looking to discover human rights dialogue one might expect to find Amnesty International somewhere on your doorstep. How does this organization accomplish this? AI is unique in that a British lawyer whose inspiring assignment was to represent two imprisoned Portuguese students that raised their glasses in a toast to freedom, chartered its beginnings as a present day NGO powerhouse (About Amnesty International 2004, 9).

Mr. Branson's, the founder of AI, had a vision in 1961 that helped to begin a human rights movement by an NGO unprecedented in recent time. For the purpose of this study, it is important to recognize a timeline of significant human rights activities and that the UDHR is the source document that AI refers to as its human rights introductory document.

AI boasts membership of nearly two million people internationally as of 2004. AI accepts no funds and does not ask for them from governments for their work campaigning against human rights violations. (About Amnesty International 2004, 9) AI has a unique mission which outlines everything from their vision to disclosure publicly of their finances. AI's mission statement reveals significant information regarding its mission and scope of purpose as an organization. AI describes itself as having a vision and a mission. That is to say that there should be a world in which every person enjoys all of the human rights embedded in the Universal Declaration of Human Rights and other international human rights standards. (Amnesty International, 2004)

So far the UDHR is there source document and it has a very broad mission statement if it is to see all of the human rights enshrined in the UDHR and "other" international human rights standards come to fruition. There are numerous human rights covenants and treaties that might be categorized as international human rights standards. This is a vague statement of mission for a gigantic NGO such as AI. Does this fact carry relevant implications? The articles in the UDHR contain rights and responsibilities for all of humanity. So which rights should get the most attention? AI claimed they accept no money from any governments or nation- states? What does that mean? How do you get your work done without cash flow? So it is private money and donations alone that make this organization work. Interestingly enough, later you will see how much influence in government that this organization appears to wield. AI has their monumental human rights to look after, as further analysis will reveal. AI recognizes that they must give explanation for their core values and place those in the decree as well. AI systems a global community of human rights defenders with the principles of international solidarity, effective action for the individual victim, global coverage, the universality and indivisibility of human rights, impartiality and independence, democracy, and mutual respect. (Amnesty International, 2004) They cite with specificity, mandates such as international solidarity, effective action for individual victims, global coverage, and universality of human rights. This also includes indivisibility of human rights, impartiality, independence, democracy, and mutual respect for human rights. (Amnesty International, 2004) These eleven core values are worthy of further clarification but precise enough to be meaningful in a vague moralistic sense. AI has proclaimed numerous human rights abuse methods and core values to their organizations mission. AI intends to address governments, intergovernmental organizations, armed political groups, companies and other non-state actors. They seek to disclose human rights abuse accurately quickly and persistently. AI systematically and impartially researches the facts of individual cases and patterns of human rights abuses. These findings are public, and member's supporters and staff mobilize public pressure on governments and others to stop the abuses. AI urges all governments to observe the rule of law, and to ratify and implement human rights standards, and carries out a wide range of human rights educational activities; it encourages intergovernmental organizations, individuals, and all organs of society to support and respect human rights. (Amnesty International, 2004) Where is human rights abuse information to be made public? Would this be strictly for people who have internet access? AI has a bold mission in that it intends to, and does, confront powerful agencies such as governments, corporations, and armed groups. It would be reckless to say AI would address human rights abuses with partiality, as this is not the chosen method of human rights abuses disclosures.

Nicholas Owen, renowned for his edit of the 2001 Oxford Amnesty lectures examined a set of contemporary dilemmas for advocates of human rights. Seemingly impressed he wrote "The assumptions of contemporary human rights discourse, notably the identities of and relations between the "we" who take it upon ourselves to right wrongs and the "they" whose wrongs are to be righted." (Owen 2003, 2) As the editor of Human Rights Human Wrongs in support of Amnesty International, Owen recognizes an important issue to discuss at the committee gatherings in 2001. He goes on to say that "however it is now becoming clear that while such abuses have hardly ceased, many of the modern problems of human rights arise not where the state is to strong, but where weak and internally divided states cease to be able to guarantee social order." (Owen, 2003, 2) This is a reaffirmation of what I have already mentioned in an earlier chapter.

Owen goes on to talk about AI's activists and talks about "AI's success's through the good offices of third parties through harder forms of intervention such as the deployment of peacekeepers, the arming of proxies and perhaps even coercive military occupation." (Owen 2003,

3) The mission and scope of a giant NGO such as Amnesty International is a maze of international relations policies and human rights interpretation. Amnesty Internationals mission and scope of purpose listed on their internet website at the time of this research in 2004, listed specific activist campaigns for human rights violations. AI categorized these as current, active, and closed appeals. Current appeals are the same as active for purposes of this analysis. Appeals for action, urgent action networks, and worldwide appeals comprise the majority headings of their activist campaign activity.

AI "appeals for action" consist of written correspondence to nation-state decision makers to disclose an identified human rights abuse within that particular country or territory. All of their members receive an email regarding the violation and are asked to endorse documentations and letters to those individuals that should respond to the violations of human rights. "Urgent action" network information techniques apply rapid letter writing, faxes, and phone calls on behalf of those individuals in immediate short-term danger of human rights violations. On 19 March 2003, the Urgent Action technique reached its 30th anniversary. Over the years, tens of thousands of Amnesty International supporters have sent letters, faxes or emails on behalf of those in immediate short-term danger of human rights violations. (AI 30 years of Urgent Actions, 2004) "Worldwide appeals" are current or closed respectively. AI uses this terminology to describe the status of appeals they handle. AI sees this as a useful way to keep track of pending appeals and those that they have had success making a positive change. Worldwide appeals for this book were dated

1995 through 2004. (AI Act Now, worldwide appeal, 2004) Closed appeals on their site listed in the same range dated from June 1995, through June 2004.

AI's 2004 campaign listed 12 broad human rights topics. These topics ranged from violence against women, to a health professional network. Previous campaigns ranged in date from 2000-2003 and many may be outdated and are for reference purposes only. (AI Campaigns current Campaigns, 2004) What incredible work this NGO had done for the time period I had studied. Their internet web site has been meticulously updated, was polished and crystal clear for easy access and understanding. Activist campaigns to thwart human rights abuses were divided as worldwide appeals and campaigns categorically, but in general, the campaigns and appeals do not coincide with precise language found within the Universal Declaration of Human Rights. This is the source document for comparison of human rights categorically as determined by AI's proclamation. This was troublesome as this was unlike the definition's set forth by the UDHR. AI has had several campaigns and appeals not expressly defined with UDHR terminology. Some examples found on their official internet website that would not coincide with the UDHR in my opinion were the current campaign to control arms, treaty body's participation, and those companies and international financial institutions are strictly accountable for the human rights impact of their activities. (Amnesty International, 2004)

These relate more to legal definitions for organizations that have evolved since the inception of the UDHR. However, several campaigns, and appeals do relate directly to the UDHR in language and in intent. AI country campaigns consist of human rights language such as asylum, refugees, torture, false imprisonment, freedom of expression, execution of minors, prisoners of conscience, and illegal detainees. These are all well within the scope of human rights language found in the UDHR. I make this decision because it is important to consider whether significant definitions of human rights have been reinterpreted, or are they in strict compliance with definitions first set forth by the monumental proclamation?

In the case of AI, some significantly different human rights activist campaigns have surfaced while some older notions of human rights announced in the UDHR remain consistent with the language and scope. Whether there will be legal, moral, or otherwise internationally significant implications, such as trend setting, the spillover effect, or a completely new set of human rights crises for other human rights NGOs, may become a renewed consideration for researchers and analysts alike.

VI

Human Rights Watch Activism, Getting it done!

Human Rights Watch (HRW), an NGO formerly referred to as Helsinki Watch began human rights protection and advancement in 1978. Human Rights Watch describes itself as an NGO with more than 150 dedicated professionals employed internationally. These professionals consist of lawyers, journalists, academics, and country experts. It is common that HRW join forces with another NGO to further common goals. HRW boasts that they are the largest human rights organization based in the US. (Human Rights Watch, 2004)

According to their official website, it is the intent of HRW to generate extensive coverage in local and international media. This publicity helps to "embarrass abusive governments" in the eyes of their citizens and the world. When embarrassment is not enough, HRW presses for the withdrawal of military and economic support from governments that egregiously violate the rights of their people. (Human Rights Watch, 2004) HRW does not indicate who they will press but the implications do point to the United States or the United Nations.

HRW began its mandate in 1978 as Helsinki Watch. At that time, the primary goal was to monitor the compliance of Soviet bloc countries with the human rights provisions of the landmark Helsinki Accords. HRW explains further that by 1988 the "watch" groups had assembled a committee to form the present day international human rights group. This group has a new internationally flavored mandate for human rights abuse identification. HRW also displays significant influence to encourage economic and military sanctions upon violating governments. HRW has a main office in New York with international organizations in Brussels, London, Moscow, Honk Kong, Los Angeles, San Francisco, and Washington. HRW in 2004 had operations and "developments" in 70 countries. HRW believes that international standards of human rights apply to all people equally, and that sharp vigilance and timely protest can prevent the tragedies of the twentieth century from reoccurring. (Human Rights Watch, 2004) HRW uses the "international standards" language to describe its mandate, but loosely termed, this can create some discourse as to what exactly are "international standards" of human rights. HRW see the hallmark and pride of HRW is the even-handedness and accuracy of their reporting. Just like Amnesty International, they do not accept financial support from any government or government funded agency. (Human Rights Watch, 2004) HRW receives donations from private organizations and from private individuals only. Interesting so this would make one wonder what are the donors priorities to further such a huge organization? I am perplexed how this organization gets this job done with private donations, perhaps they also strive to work with government grants? I will look into this as they are eligible to work with government grant funding as a non-governmental organization. HRW has wielded tremendous governmental influence as you will see from my content analysis in the upcoming tables. Human Rights Watch is a formidable NGO as evidenced by their former mission to literally be a government spy on the former Soviet bloc. One should not underestimate this organizations influence or persuade in the arena of human rights abuse identifications, corrections, and enforcement. Human Rights Watch mission and scope of purpose is one in which they believe that "international standards" of human rights apply to all peoples equally, and that sharp vigilance and timely protest can prevent the tragedies of the twentieth century from reoccurring. (Human Rights Watch 2004) This statement reflects with accuracy what HRW intentions are and why they exist. The 2003 Human Rights Watch World Report further clarifies the official internet website mission statement. "Human Rights Watch defends freedom through expressing due process and equal protection of the law, and a vigorous civil society, to document disappearances, torture, arbitrary imprisonment, discrimination, and other abuses of internationally recognized human rights." "Our goal is to hold governments accountable if they transgress the rights of their people." (Human Rights Watch 2003, vii)

The authors of their mission statement realize that it does not limit HRW in any way as to what "international standards" of human rights they intend to address nor does it place burdensome limits upon the organizations methods or legal basis to proclaim itself a human rights NGO. HRW knows what sharp vigilance and timely protest can accomplish as long as the organization and the world also know what this entails. Their continuous mission seems highly likely to continue to be accomplished. When HRW conducts activist campaign you can be most certain that nearly all human rights issues that cut across national boundaries were defined on their website in 2004. These included academic freedom, Aids, arms, caste discrimination, child soldiers, children's rights, corporations, drugs, free expression, human rights defenders, and the International Criminal Court. Furthermore, international justice, labor rights, lesbian and gay rights, freedom of the press, prisoner treatment, racism, refugees and repressions, United Nations, and women's rights round out an unbelievably extensive list.

HRW distinguishes economic, social, and cultural rights from the previous list of human rights issues. This is a large mandate to be active towards identification and reporting. The research suggests that because of the vastness of their proclaimed mandates, HRW has an endless supply of human rights protection to contend with in the future. Obviously, this analysis suggests that some of these issues again do not fit neatly into UDHR definitions of human rights abuses. This is not necessarily troublesome or a problematic finding, but is indicative of support for my hypothesis. In their publication Human Rights Watch, some other examples are listed as academic freedom, AIDS, arms, corporations, drugs, free expression on the internet, human rights defenders, and "opportunism watch" the repression in the name of anti-terrorism.(Human Rights Watch 2004, 1)

HRW has a take action campaign and it nearly mirrors the process used by AI. When a human rights abuse situation is alleged to be occurring, they send emails to all members and urge them to fax, call, or email the appropriate decision makers on behalf of the various countries. This also includes sending email and faxes directly to the US Whitehouse in Washington D.C. HRW has outlined accurate information about various countries human rights records to include Africa, the America's, Asia, Europe, Central Asia, Middle East, North Africa, and the United States. In 2004, the active campaigns included countries such as Cairo, United States, Chechnya, Uganda, Pakistan, Uzbekistan, West Africa, Afghanistan, and Nigeria. Burma, Russia, Morocco, Israel, Palestine, Saudi Arabia, Canary Islands, China, and Mexico also rounded out a very diverse grouping of countries. Another interesting observation in this analysis is that the United States is also on record for abuses of human rights. Reporting this could be a strength for their organization as well as a possible chink in its armor. Regardless, HRW activism campaigns are every bit relevant to the salient issues of the state of democratization in the world. Kenneth Roth, executive director of Human Rights Watch assessed activist successfulness; "clarity is best achieved when misconduct can be portrayed as arbitrary or discriminatory rather than a matter of purely distributive justice" (Roth 2004, 63) The director summarizes in the abstract of his journal publication that the methods employed by HRW must be able to counter the argument of distributive justice often cited by nations frequently cited for human rights abuses. HRW has a unique self-definition of human rights. As mentioned previously, HRW specific focus is on self-identified particular human rights abuse issues. HRW is dedicated to protecting the human rights of people around the world. Specifically their creed and their stance is one in which they claim to stand with victims and activists to prevent discrimination, to uphold political freedom, to protect people from inhumane conduct in wartime, and to bring offenders to justice. They claim "We investigate and expose human rights violators and hold abusers accountable. We challenge governments and those who hold power to end abusive practices and respect international human rights law. We enlist the public and the international community to support the cause of human rights for all" (Human Rights Watch World Report 2003, preface) This is with regard and in accordance with "internationally accepted" human rights mandates. The difficulty for the political scientist analyst is deciding exactly what that means. How important is the specific content of the language cited on their website or in there publication when they make their case for some human rights violations is uncertain. However, it is certain that the original mandate, the Helsinki accords, gave them US governmental backing and support to police the former Soviet bloc for human rights abuses in 1978. Their mandate was a mixture of rights abuses at that time.

The evolution of this organizations mission and self-definition is sometimes assuming from a legal but not necessarily a moral point of view. A scholarly analysis reveals clearly one fact with great certainty; that HRW is all too familiar with the human rights legal "machinery" and is ready to identify and police human rights abuses around the world.

VII

Human Right First
Activism, Getting it Done!

Human Rights First (HRF) is the third NGO I chose and with good reason for this book. They are a powerful legal resource for human rights abuse offenders to have to deal with. "Human Rights First are active in the US and internationally working diligently to create a secure and humane world, by advancing justice, human dignity, and respect for the rule of law." (Human Rights First 2004, 1) This is HRF specific definition of their organizational mission according to their official internet website as of 2004 analysis. Furthermore, according to the Critique of the 1994 Department Of State (DOS) Country Report published by HRF in July 1995, "HRF support human right activists who fight for basic freedoms and peaceful changes at the local level, protect refugees in flight from persecution and repression, help build a strong international system of justice and accountability, and make sure human rights laws and principles are enforced in the United States and abroad."

(Human Rights First 2004, 1) This is Human Rights First; formerly known as Lawyers Committee for Human Rights mandate.

This civil rights oriented NGO powerhouse's perspective on human rights, is without question one of legal significance of primarily civil human rights abuses. The essence of the mission at HRF rests in the notion that the United Nations Declaration of the Protection for Human Rights Defenders dated on the 50th anniversary of the UDHR is a milestone to realizing human rights on the ground in domestic human rights abuses situations. The reasoning behind this notion is not complex. If human rights defenders are "safe" on the ground, they can make accurate reports and put into gear the necessary mechanisms to enhance the abilities of Human Rights First to document human rights abuses. Kofi Annan of the United Nations spoke eloquently, "The declaration rests on a basic premise that when the rights of human rights defenders are violated, all our rights are put into jeopardy and all of us are made less safe." (Annan 1998) HRF would like to document, expose human rights violations, and hold governments accountable, by seeking remedies for victims and educating populations on their human rights. "These individuals commonly referred to as human rights defenders play a crucial role in combating violations and improving human rights." (Annan, 1998) This extremely efficient committee conducts further fact finding missions and publishes reports which serve as a starting point for sustained follow-up work. HRF truly pulls no punches when placing activists and defenders on the ground to gather information. They are swift to deploy whatever lawful resources essential to advance the mission as a rock solid NGO in the war against human rights abuses.

Not only has the United States been cited in congressional resolutions and by Human Rights First, but several other countries were being "monitored" by human rights "defenders" on the ground at the time of this research in 2004. The list according to their official website contained 18 countries. These were: China, Columbia, Egypt, Ethiopia, Guatemala, Haiti, India, Israel, Palestinian territories, Jordan, Kuwait, Mexico, Northern Ireland, Singapore, South Korea, Tunisia, Turkey, and Zimbabwe.

Furthermore according to HRF's publication Critique and review of the Department of State Country Reports on Human Rights Practices, "Its work is impartial, holding each government to the standards affirmed in the International Bill of Human Rights, including the right to be free from torture, summary execution, abduction and "disappearance"." (Critique, Review of the US DOS Country Reports on Human Rights Practices for 1994, 1995, 307)

Media alerts available via there official website, contained activist efforts that archive activist information dating 1996-2002. Summarily, activist programs depend primarily upon the actions of human rights defenders on the ground, however, the most salient topic for HRF are of a legal, judicial, and civil rights nature. These topics included asylum, Africa, Asia, Europe, Freedom of Association, Latin America/Caribbean, Middle East/North Africa, International Justice, International Financial Institutions, International refugees, and the United Nations. (Human Rights First sitemap, 1994, 1) Various other new and innovative representations of detailed activism information are available primarily via the use of electronic newsletters. This invaluable information is made available via internet email to HRF members and their constituents and donors worldwide. This activist method represents another invaluable means of calling attention to various governmental decision-makers in various countries. "Rights wire" is HRF first free electronic newsletter, and was published bi-weekly. "Rights Wire provides analysis of timely human rights abuses and opportunities to take action on them." (Human Rights First Rights wire 2004, 1) Human Rights First is indeed a well organized legal team of country experts and human rights defenders. This organizations mission is similar to the other two organizations I chose for this book yet distinctly different in that their focus is primarily on the civil rights and they do offer a means for reparations and compensation for those human rights abuses in which monetary means of compensation are available. This organization is invaluable to those that would need their attention and within their international lawyers arms reach.

HRF would like to see a secure world with the rule of law being enforced internationally. They would like to advance the rule of law for human rights not only internationally, but also in domestic territories of nation-states everywhere. HRF will rely upon a countless number of treaties and political activism to utilize the law and hold accountable under the law, those that would otherwise go unpunished for human rights abuses. This is no easy mandate for any organization. To seek justice for all, through the shore up and strengthening of international systems of justice and all while ensuring universal accountability for everyone. This is indeed a monumental mission.

Given the primary mission of HRF they are an NGO to be respected, to be aware of their goals, and you should be prepared to manage your human rights abuses appropriately, which is to say, not allow them to occur whatsoever. HRF utilizes as its strength the provisions set forth in various United Nations covenants and treaties to expose human rights violations, and to hold those responsible accountable.

Generally, this would mean through reparations and monetary remedies. There are resolutions and significant monetary sources available to punish human rights offenders and reward HRW's legal teams. This can mean a significantly new meaning and call for urgency to better prepare legal precedents, to establish the judicial machinery necessary under international law, and to hold countries governments culpable. Therefore these governments are held liable for human rights abuses that have occurred because of that nation-states lack of regard for international laws.

Human Rights First is indeed a formidable NGO ready to make those responsible for human rights abuse strictly accountable. HRF relies upon the definitions of human rights set forth under the UDHR, and international law. They are organized and prepared to recognize all legal machinery necessary to further their organizational goals. HRF emphasize the international justice system and domestic civil rights human rights abuses and their resolution. However, HRW disagree with countries that are not in favor of an International Criminal Court which included the US in 2004.

HRF feels those country-based tribunals are highly

effective to try international crimes and are adamantly for the International Criminal Court establishment. Weakened state sovereignty principles appear to take less precedence to the mission than individual legal and civil rights. The obvious implications for violators of human rights, by NGO human rights enforcement tactics employed by HRF set brand new case precedents. These tactics may be the new trend towards holding countries accountable to remedies under binding treaties and the UDHR, and the United Nations legal machinery. No country would wish to pay reparations and or fines for violating human rights. Those countries are accountable due to human rights protections through efforts by this well-prepared and organized NGO.

While addressing HRF accomplishments for the previous year, HRF boast of situations akin to upholding the rights of refugees, pro bono legal work for asylum seekers, and domestic abuse asylum seekers given the right to asylum. HRF has also advocated for fairness for non-citizens. Other activist efforts included huge accomplishments such as the termination of Operation Liberty Shield, and a special registration program for Arab males in the 16-25 year-old range authorized by federal law changes that conceded some registration waivers. (Human Rights First Our Accomplishments 2004) HRF has also prided itself through exposing mistreatment of non-citizens, as well as two rights positions at the Department of Homeland Security. (Human Rights First Our Accomplishments, 2004)

HRF legal accomplishments continued to be impressive and included law and security issues in the US. The organization was careful to document rights-erosions post

9/11 in two publications entitled Imbalance of Powers and Assessing the new Normal. (Human Rights First, Our Accomplishments 2004) Because HRF mandate involves complex legal issues combined with human rights and the justice system, it is no surprise how this organization can infiltrate and identify human rights abuses. The expertise is especially evident with abuses of civil human rights nature in the domestic US and abroad. Other significant activist activity has had a positive legal impact in a wide array of civil matters. In addition, HRF claims to have helped to improve the US State Departments Human Rights reporting, and protect the privacy of law-abiding citizens that helped to prohibit congressional funding for the Total Information Awareness, (TIA) program. This anti-terror initiative was a widely debated Pentagon reaction to terrorism that would have allowed the collection by the US government of personal Information of American citizens. These include driving records, tapes from airport surveillance cameras, high school transcripts, book purchase, medical records, phone conversations, and e-mails. (Human Rights First, Our Accomplishments, 2004) HRF successes were not limited to domestic civil rights initiatives, though. A prominent Egyptian human rights defender abroad was alleged to be a victim of false accusation in Egypt. Saad Ibrahim is a human rights defender based in Egypt. HRF sought US assistance and he was out of jail sooner than he had anticipated. (Human Rights First, Our Accomplishments, 2004) A Malaysian activist was out of prison after HRF intervened on his behalf. He had spent two years imprisoned because of his role as a labor rights activist in Malaysia. (Human Rights First, Our Accomplishments, 2004)

Although this is not an all-inclusive listing of HRF accomplishments in a given year, it is descriptive of the civil and judicial nature of the human rights that HRF seeks to ensure. I expect that you will find Human Rights First a worthy NGO capable of great feats and accomplishments. Arguing from legal standpoints regarding human rights, HRF is especially prepared to defend human rights abuses in a swift and efficient manner with a powerful legal team anywhere in the world.

VIII

Getting the Message, the United States Congress Responds

Because the United States, the largest military force in this world today, has such a significant role in identifying and perpetuating the successfulness of human rights initiatives at home and abroad, its mission is a very important one with numerous implications. The US Congress, via the power of the purse, is important to an NGO to lobby for human rights reforms. Because of the advent of democratization and globalization, various international relations theories have developed modern human rights, as outlined in the UDHR, which is actually just over 60 years old now. The importance and relevant significance to international relations is partially revealed by the following tables which show how Congress responds to human rights abuses internationally. Significant implications to US foreign policy regarding human rights today are based on these research findings. The door is also open to build upon this research seen as well as previous decade's foreign policy events. You should discover that my findings show a nexus between NGO efforts, and congressional resolutions which have dictated foreign policy straightforward through the 1990s and the 2000s.

In my efforts to discover theses implications, how they can be utilized and by whom, I discovered many new horizons. Nevertheless, what I also discovered irrevocably is that human rights theory is static and too reliant upon international relations theory which changes from country to country. Additionally, it is clear that the US Congress does pay close attention at least through the introduction of resolutions, to these three NGOs work. This is very important information to have qualified and organized neatly.

Nevertheless, the title of this chapter talks about the US Congress and how they speak up, so let's proceed with the preliminary findings. The following tables contain US congressional resolutions relating to the specific terminology that included human rights in the speech of the resolution "directly". The usefulness of this analysis is through comparison. I theorize that if you identify specific countries human rights violations, and trends, you can measure successes and or shortcomings of NGO activism. In this research US congressional resolutions provide compelling evidence of NGO activism regarding human rights issues and country abuses of them. The other consideration is that an identification of an abuse is a success while a cessation of abuses would be a great success. Better yet, if a country is not cited ever again, than you have an extremely great success. Furthermore, with new and powerful NGO human rights machinery and salient discourse internationally, the US response mechanisms found in the congressional responses help to assess United Nations human rights effectiveness as well. The doctrine of deterrence is also a considerable notion of human rights abuse prevention success. Therefore, there are intervening variables to consider and acknowledge when attempting to make a positive correlation between NGO activism, US political or policy response, and cessation of human rights abuses. Another important consideration is to examine how a nation is cited. If it is cited again the next session of Congress, it only makes sense that for some reason or another, that human rights abuse or a different one continues to exist. This is simple enough to follow along with. You will see that some nations will be mentioned one time for a certain abuse then not mentioned the next session. The same country will show up again in another session of Congress later on. So you have to keep your eyes on the different countries and what they are being cited for to get an idea or look for country abuse identification trends. The specific language is unedited language or hints of human rights abuses found within the resolutions. These tables are extremely significant for this comparative content analysis. The information is readily available and was paramount to my research. All congressional data was compiled from (Thomas Information on the Internet, 2004).

TABLE I
Human Rights Country Report
Human Rights Congressional Resolutions
101st Congress (1989-1990)

Country/Region	Human Rights Abuse
Baltic's	human rights
Bulgaria	Turkishminority oppression
Burma	human rights
China	one child family, Tiananmen Square,
Cuba	request for plebiscite, egregious human rights
EL Salvador	reduce human suffering
East Europe countries	human rights
Ethiopia	commit to human rights, discriminate against Jews
Guatemala	peaceful end to 30 - year civil war
Honk-Kong	human rights
Haiti	human rights
Iran	Ba ha' I persecution
India	Punjab region
Iran	human rights
Kenya	deteriorating human rights
Liberia	human rights
Laos's	human rights
Malaysia	human rights
Malawi	basic human rights

Nepal	human rights
N. Ireland	employment practices
Paraguay	human rights/civil liberties
Poland	human rights
Romania	human rights
S. Africa	detained children
Taiwan	human rights, democratic reforms
Tibet	denial of asylum seekers
UK	human rights

TABLE II
Human Rights Country Report
Human Rights Congressional Resolutions
102nd Congress (1991-1992)

*asterisk indicates country cited by previous Congress

Country/Region	Human rights Abuse
Burma*	"horrifying abuse", trafficking
China*	Illegal detainees, workers' rights, extra judicial killing, torture, civil remedies, political prisoners, prison labor, involuntary sterilization, coercive abortion
Cuba*	human rights violations
East Timor	human rights violations,
India	illegal detention, human rights violations
Iran*	Ba ha 'I repression
Iraq*	protection of refugees, minority suffering, i.e. Kurds, international recognition of human rights, genocide, war crimes rights violations, political human rights
Kenya*	political human rights
Mauritania	human rights abuses
N Ireland*	human rights abuses
Romania*	anti-Semitism, human rights against Hungarians, ethnic intolerance

Russia	illegal detainees
S. Africa*	apartheid
Somalia	human rights
Sudan	human rights violations
Taiwan*	peaceful political change
Thailand	human rights violations
Tibet*	human rights/freedoms
Uganda	human rights
United Kingdom*	violence against Ireland
Vietnam*	political prisoners
Yugoslavia	human rights
Zaire	democracy/human rights abuse

TABLE III
Human Rights Country Report Card
Human Rights Congressional Resolutions
103rd Congress (1993-1994)

No specific country listed as subject of resolutions: ratify United Nations Covenant on the Rights of the Child, healthcare, fundamental human rights, human rights for all women, displaced persons assistance, rights for those with disabilities, ratify CEDAW, Iraqi* war crimes.

***asterisk indicates country was cited
in previous years Congress**

Country/Region	Human Rights Abuse
Bosnia	mass rapes
Burma	trafficking of women
Chile	workers' rights, victims of torture
China	recognize international human rights, food and medical care as basic human rights
Guatemala	human rights
Haiti	human rights abuses
India*	detention laws, healthcare for women and children
Indonesia*	support NGO of human rights
Kashmir*	human rights
Malawi	oppression, disabilities worldwide
Mexico	free and fair elections

Middle East	condemn terrorism
Northern Ireland*	human rights
Sudan*	tragic human atrocities
Tajikistan	human rights
Vietnam*	political asylum seekers, human rights democracy, religious liberty, protect indigenous people, prohibit involuntary return of refugees, political prisoners, and multi-lateral peace activities
Yugoslavia*	systematic rapes
Zaire*	international terrorism, slavery, democracy

TABLE IV
Human Rights Country Report Card
Human Rights Congressional Resolutions
104th Congress (1995-1996)

A specific country not a subject of resolution: Stop persecution of Christian's worldwide, interstate enforcement of child support; ratify CEDAW, human political rights, slavery.

*asterisk indicates country cited by previous Congress

Country/Region	Human Rights
Bosnia*	trafficking of women, political freedoms, human rights
Burma*	trafficking of women, political freedoms, human rights
Cambodia	genocide
Cameroon	human rights
China*	child labor, human rights, religious detainees
Greece	Greek civilians slaughter red during WWII
Haiti*	human rights
India*	human rights
Kenya	political/human rights
Kosovo	political/social rights
Mauritania	chattel slavery/establish living wage
Sudan*	chattel slavery

Thailand	human trafficking/political rights
Turkey	human rights
USA	human experimentation, protect internationally recognized human rights
Vietnam*	release political prisoners, illegal prisoners
Yugoslavia*(former)	human rights

TABLE V
Human Rights Country Report Card
Human Rights Congressional Resolutions
105th Congress (1997-1998)

*asterisk indicates country cited
by a previous Congress

Country/Region	Human Rights Abuse
Afghanistan	human rights, humanitarian situation
Belarus	fundamental freedoms, rights, trafficking women
China*	trafficking transplanted organs, human rights, Tibetan prisoners
Croatia	human rights
Cyprus	human rights abuses, recommitting to the 50th anniversary of the UDHR
Ecuador	human rights, due process
Germany	religious freedom
Guatemala	human rights
Honduras	child labor, human rights
India*	human rights
Japan	WWI war crimes
Mauritania	chattel slavery, establish living wage
Sudan*	chattel slavery
Thailand	human trafficking/political rights
Turkey	human rights

USA	human experimentation, protect internationally recognized human rights
Vietnam*	release political prisoners, illegal prisoners
Yugoslavia*(former)	human right

TABLE VI
Human Rights Country Report Card
Human Rights Congressional Resolutions
106th Congress (1999-2000)

***asterisk identifies country or region
cited by a previous Congress**

Country/Region	Human Rights Abuse
Afghanistan*	women/children human rights abuses
Belarus*	child soldiers, discrimination
Burma	human rights
Central Asia	"non-compliance human rights"
China*	political rights, fair open trials, human rights
Columbia	speed the peace process
Cuba	violation of human rights
Cyprus*	human rights
El Salvador	war crimes
Eritrea	human rights
Germany*	freedom of religious beliefs
Guatemala*	recognize human rights
Haiti	free elections
Honduras*	human rights
India*	human rights abuses
Iran	anti-Semitism
Kosovo*	refugees
Kuwait	women's suffrage

William Manosh

Laos's	human rights
Mexico	political repression
Peru*	freedom of the press
Russia	freedom of the media/press
Sierra Leone*	violations of human rights
Sudan*	genocide/terrorism
Vietnam*	human rights
Yugoslavia*	political prisoners

TABLE VII
Human Rights Country Report Card
Human Rights Congressional Resolutions
107th Congress (2001-2002)

***asterisk indicates country or region
cited by previous Congress**

Country/Region	Human Rights Abuse
Afghanistan*	human rights for women, torture, freed of religion
Africa	democracy/human rights
Belarus*	refugee flight, torture
Central Asia*	human rights
Chechnya	human rights violations
China*	disc gays/lesbians, child soldiers, inheritance rights
Congo	transition to democracy
Cyprus*	community rights
Cuba*	political prisoners, honor killings, declassify exec docs
East Timor	war crimes
Europe	religious tolerance
Iran*	rights of women, democracy
Italy	illegal detainees
Japan	illegal persecution, "Comfort women during WWII"
Kazakhstan	execute by stoning, sex exploitation, democratization
Lao's*	executions

Pakistan	freedom of religion
Palestine	persecutions
Russia*	strengthen democracy, freedom of the media
Serbia	wrongful imprisonment
Turkey	ethnic conflict, freedom of religion
Ukraine	free speech and assembly
USA	torture
Uzbekistan	protects democracy, train Muslims on human rights
Vietnam*	torture victims
Zimbabwe	human rights, international law

TABLE VIII
Human Rights Country Report Card
Human Rights Congressional Resolutions
108th Congress (2002-2003)

No specific country listed: establish international women's day, ratify CEDAW, condemn execution by stoning, establish an international tribunal

***asterisk indicates country cited
by a previous Congress**

Country/Region	Human Rights Abuse
Africa*	recognize the descendants slave trade, inherit rights
Afghanistan*	security for women and children
Belarus*	fair elections, human rights, rule of law
Burma	human rights conflicts
Central Asia*	human rights
China*	oppression of humans, prisoners of conscience
Cuba*	political prisoners, poor human rights
France	freedom of religion
Hong Kong	"need for freedom"
India	child labor
Indonesia	end human rights abuses
Iran*	religious freedom, rights of women

Iraq	prosecution of Iraqi war criminals
Israel	solidarity with US in war against terrorism
Japan*	acknowledge "comfort women" WWII
Kosovo	consolidate democratic self-government
Lao's	religious liberty, democratic reform, freedom
Libya	ceasefire in civil war for democracy
Mexico	illegal killings
N. Ireland	human rights and violence
N. Korea	respect human rights, promote human rights
Russia*	comply with democracy if member of G8
Rwanda	remember victims of genocide of 1994
Saudi Arabia	human rights, absence of freedom of religion
Syria	violations of human rights
Sudan*	attacking civilians, abolish slavery
Turkey*	release political prisoners
Ukraine*	promote democracy
USA*	detainees from Afghanistan, Iraq, establish living wage

The United States congressional resolutions presented in these tables represent with little doubt the fact that Congress seriously consider human rights not only in domestic policy situations, but in all nations and territories without exception. Democratic institutions such as the US Congress are proud agencies with strong moral and legal obligations to protect their constituent's interest as well as international interests which affect domestic policy. They are integral agents of United States foreign policy through the "power of the purse". The Congress has a duty to introduce and establish while the executive branch will enforce US policy abroad. Because of this domestic accountability, by default the United States will be held accountable by the rest of the world for human rights abuse enforcement and compliance as other nations are also expected to comply with a unipolar nation state like the US's human rights abuse compliance precedents. This awesome power and influence is an assumed responsibility to lead and support human rights which is what Americans would want anyway. For the United States, it appears for now that this process has been rolling, to begin with congressional resolutions which are hoped to eventually form international relations policies and possibly new human rights abuse legislation.

The methods used to quantify and qualify the data gathered for were comprised mainly of comprehensive comparisons of NGO activism campaigns and US congressional resolutions. The information relating to the NGOs were available on each NGOs official websites. I analyzed official NGO publications thoroughly to verify the accuracy of the information reported on the organizations official websites. I discovered that NGO field monitors and employees prepare human rights abuse data. Some human rights abuse data and statistics were readily available and invaluable while preparing my book as I came to discover preliminary conclusions.

The research process had taken the form of a content analysis, a popular type of political science research method. The human rights data collected from the three official NGO internet websites, NGO print publications, and the various human rights abuse congressional resolutions were exactly what I was looking for. Human rights reports and activism campaigns available on the official internet sites for each of the three respective NGOs were perused thoroughly for content. Each NGO has official print publications, which were cross-referenced for accuracy to ensure the "official" internet websites contained up to date and verifiable missions in each NGO's official print publications. These were resources such as Human Rights, Human Wrongs, and an official publication in support of Amnesty International published by Oxford University Press in 2003. In addition, I consulted a print publication by the Lawyers Committee for Human Rights entitled Critique. In this publication, a review was conducted of the US State Departments Country Reports on Human Rights practices. This book was published in 1995 by the Lawyers Committee for Human Rights (LCHR). Finally, an extensive publication by Human Rights Watch entitled World Report which was published in 2003 provided a brilliant and informative cross reference to gain information and cross reference with the internet site the mission and scope of Human Rights Watch as well as an official endorsement of their internet website addresses which is one of the most important portions of my content analysis. If the NGO made an official statement, prepared an activist campaign, or otherwise prepared a country report for the country cited to have human rights abuses occurring on their official internet website, it was a positive identification of a human rights abuse for that country in that year. The content analysis methods also closely examined the human rights language used in eight consecutive US congressional sessions. This lengthy time consuming and nearly exhausting study process allowed for further comparison of congressional resolutions for human rights issues with NGO country reports, and activist campaign respectively for analysis.

All three types of NGO activity monitoring reporting systems categorized one issue for purposes of quantifying this data. The result for analysis is a ratio or percentage of issues per congressional resolution, (IPCR). This ratio is indicative of a percent of NGO human rights issues that mirrored the same issues for that congressional session. The larger the percentage for that congressional session the more frequently the NGO is citing the same abuse as the US congress. A preponderance of NGO human rights language identifies the issues in those countries during those Congressional Sessions. Table IV represents a culmination of the findings for this content analysis and provides compelling evidence for this book to support my original thesis questions. After you review this table we can analyze in detail a bit more what it may or may not mean.

TABLE IV
NGO Human Rights Report Card by
Percentage of Congressional Resolutions

(Congressional session) #of countries Reported)

	AI	HRF	HRW
108th	AI (IPCR)	HRF (IPCR)	HRW (IPCR)
29	79%	31%	55%
107th	AI	HRF	HRW
26	81%	19%	73%
106th	AI	HRF	HRW
26	69%	31%	80%
105th	AI	HRF	HRW
24	58%	15%	67%
104th	AI (IPCR)	HRF (IPCR)	HRW (IPCR)
17	59%	no avail	53%
103rd			
18	no avail	no avail	67%
102nd			
25	no avail	no avail	80%
101st			
30	no avail	no avail	70%

*(IPCR) = (NGO human rights related issues per congressional resolutions) (percent or ratio) Calculated by adding the number of NGO mentions of specific human rights abuses per congressional session and divide by number of human rights related congressional resolutions found during that particular session.

Table IV unquestionably demonstrates clearly my original hypothesis that NGO human rights reporting has a significant correlation to congressional resolutions human rights abuse reporting. The high percentages of concurring human rights related campaigns, country reports, and activist campaigns overwhelmingly concur with the language contained in the congressional resolutions. Each individual NGO website contained comprehensive compilations of human rights information for comparison. Let's have a look at some of the trends reflected in the tables. Beginning with Amnesty International, they have no mentions on their internet site and so no mentions in the US congressional resolutions for the 101st, 102nd, or 103rd Congress. However, for the 104th Congress they have the highest (IPCR) or issues per congressional resolution of the three NGOs chosen for this book. So they were off the map, so to speak, for the first three years after the end of the cold war as far as issues that made it to congressional resolutions, but they make a super strong showing in 1995-1996. I am very curious as to why they had no human rights reported as resolutions in the US Congress until nearly five years after the end of the cold war? In that same session 1995-1996, Human Rights First had no data available on their internet site, while Human Rights Watch made a close second with the US Congress with a close percentage behind Amnesty International demonstrating 53 percent of the Issues Per Congressional Resolution(IPCR). For that particular year there were 17 countries cited by the US Congress for a human rights abuses with some type of congressional resolution. So Amnesty International, a British based NGO, in their first year of citing human rights abuses that made it to a congressional resolution, managed to dominate the US congressional resolutions with the highest IPCR ratio of the big three NGOs chosen for this book. We shall continue to look at interesting trends in this most interesting table. There are numerous profound trends indicated within this data that reflect reasons for choosing each of the three NGOs respectively. Amnesty International is the oldest human rights group and has headquarters in the United Kingdom. For the purpose of this book I was mostly interested in evaluating the relationship between these three NGOs and the US Congress. It was, however, interesting to see the emphasis the Congress had considered for each NGOs compilation of human rights information respectively. A brief comparison indicates that with the exception of the 107th and 108th congress respectively, Human Rights Watch, the US based human rights group, illustrated the most prominent issues the US Congress chose to present resolutions for in the 101st through 106th congressional sessions. I found this not to be so much of a surprise. Amnesty International had the highest percentage of issues represented in the US Congress for the 107th and 108th Congress. Why the resilience for AI in those last two sessions reported? I did find HRF did not have high percentages of salient issues for the congressional resolutions in which they reported abuses. Why did Congress not give as much credence to the civil rights NGO, HRF as it did to the other three NGOs HRW, and AI? Is there some significance related to these findings? There was not one session of Congress in which HRF led in congressional resolutions in the IPCR category. I speculated and came up with the fact that perhaps because some significance related to this finding is that HRF mandates, reflect civil and judicial related human rights issues. These issues are perhaps more appropriate for other US based governmental agencies to take action upon but are these still relevant to the scope and authority of the US Congress? HRW and AI are much more in tune with human rights issues of an international scope that are arguably in the scope and purpose of the US Congress mandate to represent larger more international issues and take action as they would see fit. In an effort to more conclusively qualify and quantify these conclusions, additional research will definitely enhance the significance of the resolutions particularly if they became laws or affected foreign policy in a measurable way. This book is really a "look back" at the 15 year period following the "end" of the cold war. So far, what we have learned, the world was far from stabilized as the communist threat had ceased. Human rights abuses seemed to be very much a part of NGO and congressional rhetoric based upon my very real findings. As many actions have occurred since this research all over the world, you may find it interesting how Congress had affected change in foreign policy and international relations due to the proposed congressional resolutions presented in these particular sessions of Congress. I am certain you will be amazed at many of the outcomes from the aggressive invasion and overthrow of a dictator in Iraq by the United States in the name of human rights abuses, to the military occupation in Afghanistan. Both of these countries were listed in the congressional resolutions repeatedly. However, so were numerous other countries. Why not any significant actions against those oppressive regimes? Did the US not have an important foreign policy at stake?

What did Amnesty International do differently to gain momentum to sway so much persuade in the US Congress in the 107th and 108th Congress? These questions are still to be answered. Did this have anything to do with the United States being cited in the Human Rights Country Report Cards for torture at Guantanamo Bay? I am unsure about this but the United States has to set the example and not be the example when we talk about human rights. The conclusions are clear however and they have been adequately proven through political science content analysis methods. There is a vast network of human rights "machinery" to use a coined phrase of a scholar mentioned earlier in this book, involved in the never-ending task of identifying, reporting and conducting research into human rights matters globally. Although it may be bold to say that these three organizations are the only groups to influence the US Congress on these matters, to refute the extent to which they are not the only groups would require additional research to quantify data from other human rights reporting agencies. However, it is still difficult to say exactly which NGO or reporting agency the Congress is referring to while excluding others that may be reporting upon overlapping information. Highly respected political scientist Van Tuijl suggests that "particularly, during the last 25 years, NGOs have contributed to and national discourse on issues of global scope, such as the eradication of poverty and the promotion of gender equality, peace, sustainable development and human rights." (Van Tuijl 1999) This is an inherent argument that does require further research to advance my conclusions further.

Analysis: So whom is really Making Important Decisions?

Human rights scholars and political scientists are particularly interested in the relationship between NGOs and government bodies not only in the US but also internationally. Two British scholars Nicholas Wheeler and Timothy Dunne indicate in there essay regarding human rights theory proclaim that it is necessary that "a critical approach to security that places human rights at the center of theory and praxis, is reflecting the fundamental indivisibility of security and human rights." (Dunne, Wheeler, 2004, 9) What they are trying to discuss are the various discourses surrounding human rights theory and practice. They place security of the nation-state right alongside the importance of nations familiarity to human rights. This is an important concept that I believe I touched upon earlier. Human rights abuses weaken a nation state. Marginalizing a nations people will without question weaken a nation and quite possibly may lead to a civil war. History has shown this to be a true statement. Without straying too far from the significance of the findings in this book, it is important to mention exactly how important security is not only to nation states, but also to international world order. Dunne and Wheeler are convinced that you cannot have security if you do not address human rights. Interesting enough, it appears that privately funded NGOs are heading up the war against human rights abuses. To me, personally, this is somewhat of a slippery political slope if you will. This discourse further strengthens the importance of the relationships between Congress and NGOs in general. The US Congress is all too aware of how human rights discourse has a negative impact on international relationships. In, the late 1970s, HRW began to monitor Russian human rights abuses the result of the famous Helsinki Accords. Their importance as an agency with monitoring and reporting prowess has grown significantly not only in scope, but also in mission and reputation to human rights protection internationally. HRF has been the rock of Gibraltar in helping to solidify and codify civil rights laws not only in the US but internationally as well. AI's mission is now very much one that can be considered very mature. AI was awarded the 1977 Nobel Peace Prize in recognition of its unique role to further human right advocacy. Michael Posner, former leader of an important NGO, who now heads up an important role at the US State Department, recognizes this in his insightful essay that several key US based human rights organizations including Helsinki Watch (Human Rights Watch, and the Lawyers Committee for Human Rights (HRF) were founded during this period. This is a significant finding to support my hypothesis and conclusion that NGO's are extremely weighty to international relations decision making for the US Congress and UN bodies internationally. Muria Kruger along with her political science co-authors further enhances this point regarding a mission to explore Norms for Commentary, "At the 2003 meetings of both the working group and the Sub-Commission, many NGOs and others made public statements in support of the Norms; including Amnesty International; Christian Aid, Human Rights Advocates, Human Rights Watch, and The Lawyers Committee for Human Rights (HRF). (Weissbrodt, Kruger, 2003, 906) Heralded for their political science knowledge on the subject, Clarke and Feinerman recognize these NGOs in a note from there essay regarding criminal rights in China. "For an excellent and well informed discussion of many of the issues and institutions mentioned only briefly here, see Lawyers Committee for Human Rights, Criminal Justice with Chinese characteristics." (New York: Lawyers Committee for Human Rights, 1993) (Clarke, Feinerman, 1995, 140) Rita Maran an authority on international relations, drafts an essay that analyzes international human rights in the US and finds "NGOs are not intimidated by powerful countries; in October of 1998, Amnesty International launched a worldwide campaign focusing on human rights abuses in the US; it came as something of a shock to a public more accustomed to AI campaigns that target other countries." "The campaign, "rights for all", added the US to the list of countries that included Turkey, China, Sudan, Indonesia, and Columbia which over the years performed extensive human rights campaigns."

(Maran, 1998, 1) Fiona Robinson speaking as an authority on Ngo action, is quoted "NGOs philosophical and practical controversies determines that "the theoretical traditions informing different kinds of rights cannot be extricated from the political agendas of states-in this case, the push from many western states towards the liberalization of trade, production and finance in the contemporary period." (Robinson, 2003, 82)My expertise tells me to back up Robinson's notion 100 percent. It is important to include her point of view because it is significant; she is inadvertently stating how Ngo philosophy is affecting nation state political agendas. As I was able to advance my findings even further in this research these social rights seem to be often a topic of concern when evaluating the significance of what types of resolutions are being included on the congressional agendas. International relations scholars and human rights scholars have given credence to these NGOs in their professional publications which lend further validity and significance to their mission. These organizations have reputations as leaders and experts in their fields. The work these agencies conduct have significant implications for international relations, international law, human rights abuse identification, global, and economic security. All too often on the ground, the "defenders" are literally in harm's way to gather the information they use to compile there lengthy and ominously important reports. The danger element for those individuals is all too often unmentioned in the human rights dissertation between state actors; and it is nearly never public dialogue. Nevertheless, the US has two large NGO's within her borders, and the other western power, the United Kingdom has Amnesty International parked in the backyard. This in itself is worthy of lengthy analysis and contains obvious implications as to the importance the west has to ensure heightened vigilance towards human rights abuses and continued democracy. According to Heiner Bielefeldt who many claims is one of the most prominent contemporary representatives of an essentialist "western" understanding of human rights, however, is Samuel Huntington, the prophet of the danger of a "Clash of Civilizations". Espousing further he goes on to say "In Huntington's global political map, human rights as well as democracy, liberalism, and political secularism, belong exclusively to western civilization." (Bielefeldt, 2000, 91) As I have emphasized earlier, human rights are often regarded as rights by international law instituted by well-intended international thinkers from a westernized point of view reeling from inhumane atrocities. Bielfeldt does not necessarily support Huntington's outline for his book Clash of Civilizations nor does he consider Huntington's human rights and western theory arguments to be accurate of how human rights should really be depicted. However, I have to tend to disagree with Heiner here and feel Huntington's book is a pretty decent depiction of the East versus West dilemma regarding many key human rights and international relations policy matters. Shannon Lindsey Blanton regarded as a prominent political scientist, indicates in her publication that "neo-liberals counter that respect for human rights and democratic governance is an important concern in US foreign policy." (Blanton 2000, 123) This enlightenment is arguably completely accurate largely evidenced by the sheer numbers of congressional resolutions found within the archives of the US Congress just over the 15 years that I had looked at ever so closely. I conclude the western human rights model is the human rights baseline while many human rights theorists compete to further the notion of universality which, however, in my opinion after thorough research, seems to present some significant difficulty as you inquiry into the meaning of human rights universality, and dissect the 5 major subtypes as outlined in the Universal Declaration of Human Rights. Furthermore, academically, it is increasingly difficult to really entitle them "universal" mostly because of the "cultural" aspect of human rights. I am not saying that those that want to call them universal should just stop doing it. It is just a complex puzzle like a rubrics cube to solve this matter. To put all nation-states on level grounds culturally, it is difficult to place human rights definitions as being the same across the board although I would certainly like to as this would be much easier to enforce for everyone. At the same time I have to be culturally relevant in terms of how each nation state sovereign views human rights or don't I? According to Lee M. Caplan's "Normative Hierarchy Theory", when human rights scholars discuss international law, the debate heats up further, despite the fact that modern international law has largely discarded the classic notion of inherent state rights, the "fundamental right" rationale has exhibited surprising resiliency." (Caplan 2003, 748) Although political human rights theory is often a matter of debate when discussing human rights in general, the underlying notions of protecting the categorized human rights from the UDHR are of utmost importance to human rights discourse and international lawyers worldwide. This notion of protection of categorized human rights and the articles from the UDHR has nation state sovereignty literally on its heels though. It is a direct spillover to the missions of the NGO's I have chosen to enhance this book. Furthermore, the fact that NGOs are based within a nation states borders indicates a countries willingness to accept human rights missions that parallel the principles of a democratic society. Their physical location is presumptuous of the importance of western international power. That is to say, there is an enormous realization of the significance of those NGO's to the concept of the ultimate importance of humanity missions, as well as the implication and role supranational and nation-state governments must take, when human rights abuses occur worldwide. It is a duty filled with quantifiable political and moralistic obligations of a democracy, to protect and represent all people everywhere. NGO's and the US Congress validate the importance of this significant notion, but have not yet met all the obvious challenges. Nevertheless, the intent and mechanisms are in place to support the UDHR and UN human rights mandates. However, there is an extreme amount of private funding influencing NGOs that is really leaving a huge question mark and a variable left unaccountable to this researcher. However, as far as nation states go, they are limited only by their willingness to go past the normal threshold of acceptable NGO human rights interference or non-interference with state sovereignty.

References

Abbreviated Version of the Universal Declaration of Human Rights. 2004. Internet. Available from: http://www.ykliitto.fi/ourcomhr/2whatare.html/ Accessed June 1, 2004

About Amnesty International, 2004. Internet. Available from: http://web.amnesty.org/pages/aboutai-index.eng: Accessed May 12, 2004

Adjei, Cyril, "Human Rights Theory and the Bill of Rights Debate", The odern Law Review. (1995): 17-36

Amnesty International Now-Worldwide Appeal, All Active Appeals.2004.Internet. Available from: http://www.web.amnesty.org/web/wma.nsf/active?openview&start=8.5 Accessed: June 1, 2004

Amnesty International, Statute of Amnesty Internatioonal. 2004. Internet. Available from: http://web.amnesty.org/web/web.nsf/print/abouta? statute-eng: Accessed June 1, 2004

Annan, Kofi.1998.UN Secretary General September 14, 1998. NGO/DPI Conference. Human Rights First Preface.2004. Internet. Available from: http://www.humanrightsfirst.org/defenders_hrd_un_declare/hrd.declare; Accessed June 1, 2004

Basler, Roy P., Speech at Chicago Illinois, July 10, 1858.

The collected works of Abraham Lincoln ed. P. 493, 1953, Internet. Respectfully Quoted: A Dictionary of Quotations. Available from: http://www.bartleby.com/73/1761.html; Accessed October 15, 2004

Bielefeldt, Heiner. 2000. "Western versus "Islamic" Human Rights Conceptions: A Critique of Cultural Essentialism in the Discussion on Human Rights", Political Theory, (Feb) 90-121

Blanton, Shannon Lindsey. 2000. "Promoting Human Rights and Democracy in the Developing World: U.S. Rhetoric versus U.S. Arms Exports". American Journal of Political Science. (Jan) 123-131

Campaigns, Current Campaigns. 2004. Internet. Available from: http://www.amnesty.org/campaign/ Accessed: June 1, 2004

Caplan, Lee M. 2003. State Immunity, Human Rights, and Jus Cogens: A Critique of the Normative Hierarchy Theory" The American Journal of International Relations. (Oct): 741-781

Clarke, Donald C. and James V. Feinerman. 1995. Antagonistic Contradictions: Criminal Law and Human Rights in China. China Quarterly 135-154

Dippel, Horst. 1996. The Changing Idea of Popular Sovereignty in Early American Constitutionalism: Breaking Away from European Patterns. Journal of the Early Republic. (Spring): 21-45

Eichelberger, Clark M. 1947. The United Nations Charter: A Growing Document, Annals of the American Academy of Political and Social Science, Volume 252, Progress and Prospects of the United Nations. (July): 97-105

E.H.C. 1950. The Declaration of Human Rights, the United

Nations Charter and Their Effect on the Domestic Law of Human Rights. Virginia Law Review (Dec): 1059-1084

Fact Sheet No. 2 (Rev.1), 2004. The International Bill of Human Rights. Internet. Available from: http://www.unhchr.ch/html/menu6/2/fs2.htm: Accessed: June 1, 2004

Finkelstein, Lawrence S. 1955. Reviewing the United Nations Charter International Organization, Vol. 9. (May) 213-231

Friedrich, Carl J. 1947. The ideology of the United Nations Charter and the Philosophy of Peace of Immanuel Kant 1795-1945. The Journal of Politics (Feb):10-30

Harris, Sydney Justin. 1989. Thoughts at Large reprinted in Ann Lander's column. The Washington Post. Respectfully Quoted: A Dictionary of Quotations. (Nov) 1979. Internet. Available from: http://www.bartleby.com/73/868.html; Accessed: October 15, 2004.

Human Rights First Sitemap,2004.Internet. Available from: http://Humanrightsfirst.org; Accessed June 1, 2004.

Human Rights Wire, 2004. Internet. Available from: http://www.humannrightsfirst.org/rights.wire.htm; Accessed June 1, 2004

Human Rights Watch, 2003 World Report, Events of 2002. November 2001 November 2002. Human Rights Watch: 2003

Human Rights Watch, Who We Are.2004.Internet. Available from: http://hrw.org/about/whoweare.htmli: Accessed June 1, 2004

Introduction to Human Rights Education, History of

Human Rights Timeline, 2004. Internet. Available from: http://www.umn.edu/humanrts/peace/peaceedu/binder2.html; Accessed: June 1, 2004

Jackson, John H. 2003. Sovereignty-Modern: A new Approach to an Outdated Concept. The American Journal of International Law (Oct): 782-802

Lauren, Paul Gordon. 1983. First Principles of Racial Equality: History and the Politics and Diplomacy In Provisions in the United Nations Charter. Human Rights Quarterly, Vol. 5 No 1, (Feb) 1-26

Lawyers Committee for Human Rights, Critique Review of the US Department of States Country Reports on Human Rights Practices for 1994. : Lawyers Committee for Human Rights

Maran, Rita. 1999. International Human Rights in the U.S.: A Critique, Social Justice, Vol. 26. (49) Internet. Available from: Questia Online Library. http://www.questia.com/pm.qst?a=cd=5001290279; Accessed June 1, 2004

Mayer, Kenneth R. and David T. Canon. 1999. The Dysfunctional Congress? The Individual Roots of an Institutional Dilemma, Westview Press

Posner, Michael. 1995. Rally Round Human Rights. Foreign Policy. 133-139

Pollock, Alexander J. 1969. The South West Africa Cases and the Jurisprudence of International Law, International Organization. Autumn 767-787

Robinson, Fiona. 2003. NGOs and the Advancement of Economic and Social Rights; Philosophical and Practical Controversies. International Relations 79-96

Internet. Available from: http://ire.sagepub.com/cgi/content/abstract/17/1/79; Copyright Sage Publications

Roosevelt, Theodore. 1926. Address at the Sorbonne, Paris France, April 23, 1910 Citizenship in a Republic. The Strenuous Life, The works of Theodore Roosevelt, National Ed: 515-516 respectfully quoted: A Dictionary of Quotations. 1989 Internet. Available from: http://www.bartleby.com/731/867.html; Accessed Oct 15, 2004

Roth, Kenneth. 2004. Defending Economic, Social, and Cultural Rights: Practical Issues Faced on International Human Rights Organization. Human Rights Quarterly: 63-73

Shaw, Albert, The Messages and Papers of Woodrow Wilson. 1924. Volume 2 p 822 Respectfully Quoted: A Dictionary of Quotations. 1989. Internet. Available from: http://www.bartleby.com/73/871.html. Accessed October 6, 2004

Tudorov, Ignatieff, Singer, Bindman, Spivak, Sereney, Sontag, Hoffman, Owen, eds. 2003. In Support of Amnesty International, Human Rights, Human Wrongs Oxford: University Press

Thomas Legislative Information on the Internet. 2004. Bill Summary and Status. 2004. Internet. Available from: http://thomas.loc.gov/bss/d101query.html; Accessed March 15, 2004

Universal Declaration of Human Rights. 2004. Internet. Available from: http://www.un.org/overview/rights:html; Accessed June 1, 2004

United Nations Human Rights Website. 2004. Internet.

Available from: http://www.un.org/aboutun/charter/: Accessed June 1, 2004

Van Tuijl, Peter. 1999. NGOs and Human Rights: Sources of Justice and Democracy, Journal of International Affairs. P 493 copyright 1999. Columbia University School of International Public Affairs, Copyright 2002 Gale Group

Weissbrodt, David, and Muria Kruger, 2003. Norms on the Responsibilities of Transnational Corporations and Other Business Enterprises with Regards to Human Rights. The American Journal of International Law, (Oct) 901-922

Wheeler, Nicholas J., Tim Dunne. 2004. We the Peoples: Contending Discourses of Security in Human Rights Theory and Practice. International Relations, 9-23 Internet. Available from: http://ire.sagepub.com/cgi/content/abstract/18/1/9. Copyright Sage Publications

About the Author

William Manosh is a 51 year old US Air Force disabled veteran who resides with his wife Cara in Rochester, Ny. He began this book while still in a Political Science program at Florida Atlantic University in Boca Raton, Florida in 2002. He holds a BA in Political Science and graduated with a 3.5 GPA. William also attended FAU for two years in a graduate program with this same major. William attended Columbia Greene-Community College in Hudson New York from 1995-1996. He was awarded an AAS degree in Business Administration and graduated with honors. William served 10 years in the Air Force from January 1985- October 1994. He has 4 children and two wonderful stepchildren.William has taught American Government at a magnet program for 10th graders in Riviera Beach, Florida. William claims other than this book, this was the most challenging and rewarding position he had ever held.